The Distinguished Business Man: What a Man in Business Can Learn from Proverbs 31

Tammie T. Polk

Copyright © 2017 Tammie T. Polk

All rights reserved.

ISBN-10: **154503155X**
ISBN-13: **978-1545031551**

DEDICATION

This book is for…

All the men who see the need to be distinguished.

All the men who endeavor to be distinguished.

All the men who understand what being distinguished is.

The men who want to be distinguished in every area of their lives.

YOU!

Here's to the Distinguished Man. May you be one, know one, and raise one!

CONTENTS

1	Purpose to be Distinguished	1
2	Your Wife's Place	12
3	Be Seen, Heard, and Felt	24
4	Build Your Business Brain	32
5	Caring for the Multitudes	37
6	Establishing Your Empire	42
7	Maintaining the Man Within and Without	46
8	Having a Go-getter Mentality	51
9	Shining the Light	58
10	Be Others Minded	65
11	Make Way for the Best	69
12	You Are What You Wear	74

13	His Empire—Her Empire	79
14	Establish Your Reputation	85
15	Be Your Own Reward	92
16	Keep Yourself In Check	98
17	Productively Busy	105
18	Crown Of His Family	110
19	No Less Than Excellence	114
20	God-Fearing Business Man	119
21	Just Smile and Wave	124

Introduction

The thoughts behind this book came shortly after I published *The Virtuous Business Woman*. I wanted to revamp the book for men, but was hesitant. First, I wanted to see if that would even be possible. Then it happened—Men started looking at my book and said that I had forgotten about them! I had three men on three different occasions and at three different events to tell me this! I even had women to start telling me that their husbands and significant others were reading right along with them.

Why Proverbs 31? Although it is written to a man from his husband's point of view, it also applies to men in a lot of areas, so keep an open mind! The Distinguished Business Man is also written from the entrepreneur's point of view, yet it's for any man in a managerial or supervisory position.

The verses are at the start of the chapter because I want you to understand the context and why it still applies to you as a man. The questions are there to help you to process the reading.

Before you start your journey, pray! This is going to be quite the eye-opening experience. I saw that as I wrote. It is my hope that you understand what is written here and are able to apply it wherever you may find yourself at this point. God Bless!

1 PURPOSE TO BE DISTINGUISHED

Proverbs 31:10- "Who can find a virtuous woman? For her price is far above rubies."

Right off the jump, I know you're wondering why I have this verse at the beginning of the chapter…

Take a moment and think about the word "virtue." What exactly is virtue anyway? Many have their own definition for this word. I prefer the one that my pastor uses. He says that virtue is having moral excellence, meaning that you make a conscious decision to do what is right and then graduate to doing what is best. This is exactly what a distinguished man endeavors to do.

A distinguished business man has, exhibits, and maintains both personal and professional integrity. Known as a man of his word, he is nowhere near perfect, but people should be speaking highly of him. Words such unfair, uncaring, uncooperative, untrustworthy, should not describe him!

A distinguished business man is truthful, fair, and firm in all business dealings. A distinguished business man is not one that cheats people, takes advantage of them, overcharges them, or undercuts them. He should not misuse nor mistreat anyone he is in business with. It not only creates problems for his business, but it also brings reproach on the name of Christ. How many times have you heard someone say something like this: "He claims to be a Christian and they have done this to me or that to me." A distinguished business man maintains a consistent testimony in all that he says and does.

A distinguished business man does what is right, even if it means losing clients, money, or business relationships. Now, this is a hard pill to swallow. In today's business world, we look for those important business connections that will help us get to the next level. Sometimes we will lay our convictions aside for the sake of the business, which can lead to trouble. This has been my experience. Last year, a business relationship ended very badly. I knew what this person was about, but I focused on national recognition from being associated with her and I did not take the stand that I needed to. When the time came to deal with the situation, I was in tears because I did not want to sever the relationship. I knew that this was not going to be another opportunity like that one. This person blasted me to the hilt and, to be honest, I deserved every bit of it. Had I taken the stand that a distinguished business man should have, things might have gone differently.

A distinguished business man is guided by the principles of God's Word, even in business. If I tried to lay out every verse in the Bible that shows how you are to run your businesses as distinguished business men, this book would be as long as a dictionary! However, I will mention one, 2

Corinthians 6:14- "Be ye not unequally yoked together with unbelievers: for what fellowship hath righteousness with unrighteousness? and what communion hath light with darkness?" Most people see that verse and think about marriage, but the same rules apply in the business world.

A distinguished business man is careful with who he links up with. Not every relationship that looks good to your business may be for your business. Do your research on people that want to link up with you. Find out who their customer base really is. Find out what causes they support. Find out to whom they donate money. Talk to other business owners who may have dealt with them in the past. See how the community around them feels about their business. How does their business concept line up with the Bible? Yes, it might seem like overkill, but knowledge is power for a reason. You just might be dodging a huge bullet.

A distinguished business man uses discernment and good judgment. This goes along with our last point. Always pray and seek God's answers before pursuing anything in your business. Ask Him to help you to weed out and see through those who may both openly and secretly seek to destroy your business. Ask Him to help you to not fall prey to their devices! There are so many business people out there today that look to take out their competition in any way possible. They may seem as though they come in peace, but their true intent is to tear your business into pieces! I am reminded of Solomon's wish when God asked him what he wanted Him to do for him. Look at I Kings 3:9- "Give therefore thy servant an understanding heart to judge thy people, that I may discern between good and bad: for who is able to judge this thy so great a people?" He did not ask for long life, riches, or anything like that—he asked for a discerning heart and wisdom so that he could lead Israel in the right way. We should be just like Solomon! Think about that for a moment.

A distinguished business man knows his value. Everyone today seems to be looking for a handout, discount or something for little or nothing! A distinguished business man understands his price and stands by it. He does not lower his prices to appease people, but shows how and why he is worth the price he gives. It is okay to have baby prices in the beginning, but do not shy away from the grown man prices that you need to have to keep your business going. I had baby prices when I started out and many people were shocked at my prices. They thought I offered way too much for way too little of a price. I was surprised myself when I started using my grown man rate and found that people actually understood why! I felt like I was moving in the right direction!

A distinguished business man prices his services fairly, but competitively. Yes, this could have gone with the last point, but I decided to bring it to its own space for a reason. Coming up with a service outline and pricing structure are two of the hardest thing any business person does. I know that first hand. When I was coming up with mine, I spent hours looking at my competitors' websites and talking directly to them. I printed out everything I could, looked at what I knew I could offer as well, came up with a basic pricing structure, and then refined it. It was not an easy process, but it was something that I needed to go through. Why?

Recently, I had a client to bring up to me that one of my competitors charged half of what I did for the same services. I smiled as I listened to her compare our services. Once she was done, I asked her to look at one very important detail—the length of time. She got very quiet. What I was charging for a year round support package, meaning that she would receive services from me for nine to twelve months, this competitor was charging for three hours of his time. Anything over those three hours had additional fees: $20 for a phone call, $5 for email communication, etc. I was not charging his that way, though I previously had a similar pricing structure. Did I lock her? Yes, I did! And it is all because I stuck to my guns and showed why and how I was the better choice.

A distinguished business man does not undervalue himself or diminish his value. This may sound like the last few paragraphs, but it is different. How? It is because value means more than money. A distinguished business man does not stoop to unfair and unethical business practices. Has anyone ever told you that you knew better than to do something or get involved with someone? They told you that you were worth more than that. They told you that you and your business are more valuable than that. And, now you have to spend time redeeming yourself and your company's reputation, which could take a very long time. You do not have time for that.

A distinguished business man knows what he can and cannot do and does not misrepresent himself and/or his limitations. One of the worst things anyone in business can do is to say that they can do something that they know they cannot do! As men, this can be difficult because the last thing you want someone to think is that you can't do something. You'll say you can do it just to keep from being ridiculed or thought of as less of a man. Do not do that to yourself!

If someone asks you to do something that you cannot do or do not offer, offer to help them find someone that they can go to in order to get that done. In the meantime, you might want to learn how to do it for the next person that comes around. Once you are proficient at whatever it is, you can offer those services to the same client if they are unsatisfied with the person that they went to after speaking to you. It is better to be honest about it upfront than to lie and lose a lot more than you thought you would have!

Lastly, a distinguished business man realizes that he has something rare and precious to offer, even in the wake of competition. You are unique. You are different. You are special. You can do something that the others cannot do at all or cannot do as well as you can. You have gifts and talents from God that are specifically designed for you to do what you are doing. You have taken the time to hone and perfect those skills. You have something that no one else has, no matter how similar you may be to them. That is not necessarily overconfidence! It could very well be the truth!

This first verse of Proverbs 31 is full of things to think about and process. Pray before answering any of the questions. Be honest with yourself. This, Gentlemen, is the first step to becoming a Distinguished Business Man!

Questions

1. What do I want to be known for?
2. Am I fair and firm?
3. Am I willing to take a stand for right, even if it costs me?
4. What scriptures do I need to keep in mind?
5. What business relationships do I need to sever or reevaluate?
6. Am I using the best business practices?

2 YOUR WIFE'S PLACE

Proverbs 31:11, 12—"The heart of her husband doth safely trust in her, so that he shall have no need of spoil. She will do him good and not evil all the days of her life."

I combined these two verses for a reason. A distinguished business man honors his wife—if he has one—even in business! First and foremost, a distinguished business man is faithful to his husband! He knows how to deal with women and keep it professional. There is no talk of him being or acting in an inappropriate manner with any woman with whom he comes into contact with inside or outside of the business environment.. He should not do anything to undermine his marriage for the sake of his business, either! If he thinks that he would hurt his wife by doing what another woman is asking his to do in return for what he needs for his business, he is not going to do it! He finds a better way to get what he needs because no other woman or business relationship is worth the one that he has with his wife!

How do you get there? Is this even possible? Yes, it is, and I'm going to tell you exactly how it's done.

Your wife should know, feel, and understand your business, the vision for it, and the vision behind it, even if you feel as though she may not fully understand it. I am a married to a business man and I am a behind the scenes type of woman when it comes to his work, but I help to keep him on the ground. I am glad to be able to do that for him. Even though I may not know all of the ins and outs of his business, there are some things that I know that I can help him with and he keeps me informed!

She understands that his business exists to help support her and their home. This is a BIG one! Despite the successes you are experiencing in your business, she should never feel like her profession is second to yours. I have run across so many who feel that because own their own business, make more, or even have a more quality clientele, that they are better than their wife and what she is doing. No wife should ever feel completely left out! Yes, she may not speak to your cause in the way you may want her to, but she is trying!

I remember when my husband asked me to leave my job. At first, I thought it was a horrible idea! But then, once I saw his workload increased, I was glad that I did. Also, my being willing to do so ended up giving me time to help him with administrative tasks that he struggled with. And to be honest, I fought with him about it because I felt like my ambitions were being put on hold, but it only led to me being able to do more and greater things.

As wives, we understand that things will start to become busier as you become more successful. Our response? Many of us still want to be contributing in ways other than the norm. I wanted to keep my hands on something and help support out family in case something happened. While he was a little irritated about that, he had to step outside of himself and realize what I was saying.

I was not trying to belittle or demean what he was doing. I was not trying to say that he would need my help, nor was I saying he would not support me. However, like most women, those thoughts were the first to come to mind.

She knows that his business is meant to sustain the household. That is hard for some to grasp a hold of, but it will keep down the conflict in your home. Let me expound on that point.

She knows that his business exists to compliment and not to compete with what she is doing nor undermine it. If your business makes more money than hers, do not rub it in! Do not point it out…matter of fact, do not even mention it! Like a man, a woman also wants to know that she's doing all that she can to help maintain the household and wants to feel that she can help carry the load from time to time. Do not get agitated if she wants to keep monies together and not split up. She may even ask you to help your home out with money from the business. Something may happen and she may have to step in financially. And, more importantly, should you have to use your business to save your home, NEVER THROW THAT IN HER FACE! I do not care how bad it gets! She needs to know that you support her. She needs to know that she can count on you…which brings me to the next point.

She should feel that your business does not exist out of malice, envy, and ill will toward her. In other words, do not just up and start something because you are mad at her. Do not start a business because you are jealous of the attention and accolades she gets in her work. Do not start a business to prove a point—that is a two-edged sword. While you may very well accomplish the success and the monetary goals that you set, something is going to happen that is going to make you see why you should not have done things the way you did. Now, I am not saying that you should sit around and do nothing while things crumble around you. I am saying that you can do it with the right heart attitude and with better intentions. She should see you as trying to provide…please understand how important that is.

She should know that any success you achieve is not going to be thrown in her face and used against her. Did we just talk about this? Yes, we did a little bit, but I wanted to say more. Women give up a lot to support their families in every facet possible! Many women have left lucrative careers to tend to their homes and that should not be taken lightly! Some women are may be unable to move up and achieve the same level of success because it would mean jeopardizing their home. It should never be said that a woman has given up, lost ambition, or anything like that because, trust me, she did it for a reason! Yes, things may get hard and you may need her to help out financially, but please know that demeaning and belittling her is not the way to get it done.

There should never, ever be a day when she comes home from work or you come in from work and the events of her day are unimportant to you. If she has something that clashes with your schedule, talk about it and see what can be worked out because it is not all about you and what you have to do all the time!

I will never forget the day I signed up for an event without checking with my husband first. I got meeting days confused and realized that I wasn't going to get home in time for him to get to work. Instead of getting angry and lashing out, he actually called his boss, told him what was going on, and was able to go in late so that I could be at my event. Now, I realize that for some of you that is a dream scenario, but it is possible! By him doing that, he showed me that what I was doing and involved in was important enough to him for concessions to be made.

Also, at one time in our life together, he worked two jobs because I couldn't help him, even though I was working. I found myself saying that I couldn't help because I didn't make enough. He didn't believe me…until he actually rode around with me one pay day. I was determined to show him that I was telling the truth about what I was saying.

We stopped, cashed my check, and got a money order for $493 to cover the cost of our daughters' daycare (they were attending the daycare where I worked). He asked me how much I had left and I said about $100, which I needed to use for diapers, wipes and formula for our youngest. After that, I had $7, which I was going to use to get something to eat. He laughed and told me that he had me on lunch and that I could quit my job because that was ridiculous!

When I wanted to go back to work, he fought it because he knew how stressed out I was before. I came home with tense shoulders and migraines every day. It got so bad that I ended up losing 30 pounds in four months and neither one of us even noticed! The rest is a story for another day. Let's get back to it.

She should not feel like she is not excluded from the business and can help. Men do not realize this one thing until they have paid someone else to do it! Think about what your wife can do and see if it can be useful in your business. If she is good to bounce ideas off of, talk to her about what you are thinking of doing. She may be able to provide a different perspective that you might not have thought about. If she is good at organizing and putting things together, let her help you with your next workshop conference, or event. If she has good computer skills, let her help you with your website, presentations, and other things you may need. If my husband thinks for one minute that I can help him, he is asking me to do it. Do not leave her out. I can't tell you how many times I've rewritten letters, helped with reports, etc.

She should know that his business is not meant to eliminate hers. She may have something else that she wants to do. She may have a secret professional goal that you might not know about. Yes, it may be frustrating; however, you have to realize that the gifts and talents that God gave her are still to be used.

I understand that many of you started your businesses or careers to help your wife. I understand that you want to alleviate some of the pressure and the stress that she is under. I understand that you want to shoulder some of the weight that is sitting on her. What I do not want you to do is to try to force her to leave what she is doing to come on board with you. While it may be a good idea right then, it may not be the right time!

Honoring your wife in your business is not always an easy thing to do, but it is the right thing to do. Your wife should never feel as though she is less of a woman because of what you are doing and you should not treat her that way. She should not have to find ways to feel fulfilled and needed because you are so set on your business succeeding. Nevertheless, that is another story for another chapter.

Look at the questions for this verse. Think about your wife. Do you need to talk through and work some things out? If so, what are they? If you know what they are, are you willing to get it right? Pray about it and move forward when you are ready to do so.

Questions

1. Do I know what my wife's strengths are? Am I using them?
2. Do I need to ask her forgiveness for anything? If so, what?
3. Do I (or am I) exclude her because of what I think she may not know or be able to help with?
4. Am I in this business to hurt her or get back at her for something?
5. Am I carrying myself in a way that makes her feel undervalued?
6. Do I let her know that she matters to me and that her input is important to me?

3 BE SEEN, HEARD, AND FELT

Proverbs 31:13—"She seeketh wool, and flax, and worketh willingly with her hands."

A distinguished business man educates himself! He takes the necessary steps to ensure professional growth for himself and growth for his business. It is beyond imperative that you stay on top of things in your realm of business. Getting caught off guard can lead to your business virtually vanishing from sight. What do I mean? Let us talk about it a while.

A distinguished business man keeps up with trends that relate to his business. That means you are paying attention to what is going on. You know what works and what does not. You are trying new approaches that may help propel your business to the next level. You are constantly reading relevant periodicals and blogs so that you can stay up on what the needs are in your world. You try new apps and other software that is meant to enhance your business. You check out any new competition. It is all about staying relevant while maintain a God-honoring business!

A distinguished business man actively advocates for and advertises his business. Do not be the best-kept secret in town! Let people know that you are out there. Let people know that you exist. Let people know what you have to offer. Let people know what makes you different. If you do not put yourself out there, you will not be out there. Having a website and social media posts alone will not do the work for you. No, sir! Start going to community events and vendor shows. You have to get out, hang flyers, and leave business cards in places where you know you can help. Join groups on social media that will help you get your name out in the way that you want it to. Network! Do not let your opportunities pass you by!

A distinguished business man attends networking meetings, conferences, and workshops that enhance his professional skills and business offerings. You will gain more than money when you do. You will have gained connections. Weird? Not really. Why? It is because you will know when the next event is, who to contact, and what you can and cannot do before you leave. You will start to meet people who were interested in what you do. You will be asked to speak to different groups. Attend any meeting that time and money will allow! Get yourself out there and get involved!

A distinguished business man sets a schedule for himself, but allows for flexibility. It is hard to keep an open-ended schedule, but it is something that you might want to think about. It is okay to have normal business or working hours, but there has to be some flexibility there! I will give you an example. My husband and I operate on polar schedules—my business is a day business and his is a night business. I have to account for that more than most because we are also homeschool parents. I have to make sure that my schedule does not keep him from getting the rest that he needs, allows for school with our girls to be done, and does not have him running late for work at night. Do we clash? Yes, and quite hard at times, but we make it work.

Do not over schedule yourself, either. Learn to say no or that you cannot do that right now. I promise you that your business will not fall apart. First and foremost, make sure that you are getting in time with God! You will have your best days when you have taken the time to read the Bible and pray. No matter what it is you read, find a way to make it relate to your day. Take the time to pray about all that you have before you that particular day. Ask God to help you to make the best decisions possible, to be there when your family needs you, and to do what is right. To many it may seem small and unnecessary, but it most certainly is not. I saw a quote on Facebook that said that if you have not bathed your business in prayer, then you are not ready for profit.

Take care of yourself. We forget that along the way. As men, you go into overdrive and often tell yourself and others that you're all right…until you're not. I remember my husband trying to go to work after being diagnosed with a concussion. He said he felt fine. He told his boss he was fine. It was hard to convince that man to stay home that night, but I understood why. He was trying to make sure that everyone had what they needed. He was trying to make sure that he could help me. He was trying to make sure that he was doing his absolute best, but he was forgetting about himself. He did not even realize that his vision was blurrier than normal. Do not spend more time investing in your business than you do investing in yourself.

A distinguished business man sets realistic, measureable, and attainable goals with definite and clear deadlines. We all have this pipe dream of what we want our businesses to be, how we want things to run, who we want to be like, who we want to be linked up with, how much money we want to make – you get the point. What are you doing to get there? Have you even made a plan yet? Have you prayed about it? Did you even write all that stuff down? Yeah, about that!

A distinguished business man is PIRRPEARed. Do you think I meant prepared? Same thing, but different letters. Let me explain. When it comes to staying relevant in the business world, you have to realize that it is a process! **Pray** about what you are doing and how to keep it going. **Investigate** ways to do what needs to be done without sacrificing way too much. **Read** everything you can get your hands on. **Research** what is new, what still works, what you need to do away with, etc. **Plan** your next course of action. **Execute** the plan you have put together. **Adapt** the plan if necessary. **Re-execute** with the new plan in mind. Does that make sense? You probably never thought about it that way!

Lastly, a distinguished business man surrounds himself with like-minded people who help him, challenge him, and keep him accountable. That is right, sir, you need a TEAM! You need to have those go-to people. These are people that you know you can call and ask for a quick prayer. These are the people you can pitch your ideas to and they will tell you that you need to rethink that. They make sure you are doing what you said you were going to do and pushing you to get off your butt and get your stuff in order—yes, you need them all! The accountability person is by far one of the most important. You need that person who will give you God's answers for the situations that you are facing. You need that person who is not afraid to tell you that what you are doing does not line up with the Bible. You need that. Iron sharpens iron.

Whew! That's was a lot in a little bit. The question for this verse are for you to get PIRRPEARed. It is time to get your life together, sir. Now, go get it!

Questions

1. Am I at the top of my game?
2. Am I teachable?
3. Do I think I know it all or already have it together?
4. Am I out there?
5. Do I have a team?
6. What are my goals?

4 BUILD YOUR BUSINESS BRAIN

Proverbs 31:14—"She is like the merchants' ships; she bringeth her food from afar."

A distinguished business man looks everywhere for resources to help his business to grow. While you may find what you need in your immediate area, do not be afraid to shop around. There may be something and someone better out there for you to do business with or link up with Yes, you may know of someone who can turn your presentation into a New York Times bestseller. However, there may be someone else who can do it quicker. Yes, you will have to pray over your stuff before you send it, but that is a part of doing business.

A distinguished business man looks at his business from all angles. There is nothing wrong with going back to the drawing board. Remember how I talked about being PIRRPEARed in the last chapter? The A and the R stand for Adapt the plan and Re-execute the plan. Revisit your business mission and vision. Does it need to be expanded? Look at your website. Is it the best representation of you and your business? Look at your blog. Don't give me that look—men blog, too!

Are you posting what is relevant and what people want to read? Look at yourself and how you handle certain aspects of the business. Are there some areas that you need to tighten up in? Where do you and your business stand with God? Is it time to do some recommitting and refocusing? These are things that a distinguished man thinks about almost on a daily basis. You may be doing well, but you can always do better.

A distinguished business man carefully considers the source of information given to him and weighs the pros and cons as it applies to the vision and goals for his business.

He makes sure that any information he receives is credible before altering his business model. He makes sure that it makes sense given the scope of his business. He is not quick to join the cause simply because it comes well-advertised and highly recommended. He dissects it because he knows that, if it fails, it is a reflection on him. He takes his time in making the decision and does not allow pushy people who put pressure on him cause him to make a rash decision. He has been there before, in most cases, and is not looking to go there again. The decisions that he has to make could propel his business to the next level or break it back down to ground zero. Not every risk is worth taking.

A distinguished business man is willing to travel both reasonable and unreasonable distances if it means that what he's looking at is going to propel his business forward. You have been there before. You see a workshop that you know is going to help you solve a problem in your business—and then you see that it is several hours away. You start to think about how you can make it happen because you know you need to be there. You know that the opportunity will probably never be available locally and you really cannot afford to miss it.

You run your numbers and see that you are going to have to get very creative in your spending to allow for travel expenses. Your team will tell you that it is a long way to go for something like that and may even try to show you something similar and closer. You know that is not going to work, so you keep pounding at it until you figure out how to make it work.

Not only will you learn what you need to do your job more efficiently, you might have a great time! Although, it is a sacrifice, You have to suck it up. Decisions have to be made.

The questions for this verse are to help you to make those decisions. There are other scriptures to consider and reflect on as well. Think about what you been told, who has been recommended to you, what you have seen lately, etc. Ask yourself this question: Is this going to help my business and how?

Questions

1. Does my business mission and vision need to be expanded?
2. Is my website the best representation of me and my business?
3. Is my blog and what I am posting relevant and what people want to read?
4. How do I handle my business? Are there areas I need to tighten up in?
5. Where do my business and I stand with God? Is it time for me to refocus and recommit both myself and my business to God?

5 CARING FOR THE MULTITUDES

Proverbs 31:15- "She riseth also while it is yet night, and giveth meat to her household, and a portion to her maidens."

A distinguished business man takes care of his family and his employees, if he has any. Notice that family is first. He takes care of home FIRST, meaning that he makes sure that his family is taken care of and is not second to his business. As hard as that can be, a distinguished business man knows when he needs to step back and attend to his family.

You may not have any employees yet, but I will say this—a distinguished business man treats his employees fairly, pays them competitively, values their work, and rewards and disciplines them with dignity and professionalism. I am going to spend the rest of the chapter breaking those down.

Treating your employees fairly is beyond important! No one wants to work for someone who does not do what they are asking their employees to do. They do not want to work for someone who is always thinking about the workload and their bottom line when they need a little time off from work. They want to work for someone who is approachable. They want to work for someone who does those little things when big events are happening in their lives and understand why those things are important to them.

A distinguished business man values the work of his employees. He does not take credit for things and ideas that his employees came up with or created. He gives credit where it is due and shares the spotlight with them. He does not take what they made and not allow them to use it elsewhere.

A distinguished business man would allow that employee to include it in their professional portfolio. You may disagree with that, but I would encourage you to give it some thought. Why? They are not stealing from the company. This is something that they create to use in the company and they should be able to reserve the right to keep it for other uses or receive compensation for it if the company wishes to keep it.

Lastly, a distinguished business man rewards and disciplines his employees with dignity and professionalism. There are times when things should be done either publicly or privately. An employee should never be disciplined publicly. It is okay to talk about what happened in a general sense; however, that person should not be paraded around for everyone to know what happened. It is okay to send out an email entailing what policies and procedures are or will be, but names should not be used.

When it comes to rewarding employees, it should be done as both a reward to them and an encouragement to others. It also should not be excessive, too frequent, nor too flashy. It also needs to be fair! Someone that has been working for you for a year should not get the same thing as someone who has been there from day one. Rewards should have differing, yet fair levels.

This also should not always be done publicly. Not everyone in the company needs to know who earned a bonus. Not everyone in the company needs to know who is getting a raise. Not everyone in the company needs to know who gets a certain position. You have to be careful with making certain things public because it could very well lead to you having issues with disgruntled employees. Be very clear about your expectations for reward and discipline alike.

Always remember that small things mean a lot. Some people do not need much. They just want to know that you know that they are doing their best. A thank you, pat on the back, nice email, or a simple congratulations—these are small things that many will appreciate.

Another thing to remember is that you cannot please everyone. Someone is going to feel that what you are doing as a reward or for discipline is not enough for them. Do not harp too much on what could have happened and what you did not have to do. That will usually add fuel to the fire. Listen to their concerns, take action, and move forward.

The questions for this verse are meant to challenge you to get some things right in these areas, to make you think, and also to make a plan! Do not take them lightly.

Questions

1. Am I making time for my family?
2. How does my business life affect my family life? Is there a balance?
3. How do I view my employees?
4. Could I be doing more for my employees?
5. Could I be doing more for my family?

6 ESTABLISHING YOUR EMPIRE

Proverbs 31:16- "She considereth a field, and buyeth it: with the fruit of her hands he planteth a vineyard."

A distinguished business man looks for the perfect place to build his business! He weighs his options of either having his main operation in his home or in a place outside of his home. Sometimes this is a hard decision to make. It really boils down to whether or not you have the space to do so and how you being there will mesh with your family dynamic. Will you be able to work uninterrupted? Will it be quiet around you? Is there an office complex within a reasonable distance of your house? These are decisions you have to make.

A distinguished business man also does not buy or rent the first place he sees! He takes his time, prays about it, and gets the space that is BEST or a stepping-stone toward the best. He also does not buy the biggest space right off and takes care not to put too much on himself in the beginning.

Once the decision is made – in the home or outside the home—a distinguished business man fashions that chosen place so that it can be at its best and allow his to serve all whom he meets. His place is professional, yes, but it is still inviting and decorated for the task. The environment your clients walk into should make them feel at ease in working with you and not make them tenser or doubt that they want to work with you. It should be comfortable and the colors and décor should be as tasteful as possible.

A distinguished business man is also wary of how much he spends. It is much better to start out with a little and then build on that instead of buying the biggest and the best up front and not having enough money left to run your business. It is not necessary to spend thousands of dollars decorating an office! And, don't be too proud to ask for help, either!

In his fashioning, a distinguished business man makes sure that his environment allows for growth to be made and success to be attained. Neither he, his employees (if any), nor his clients should be limited by the size and furnishings in the building. They should walk in there and feel as though they are going to get something done! The artwork on the walls should be inspiring and not just informational. The colors should be intriguing to the eye, but not flashy. When the décor is too out there, people do not take you seriously at all. On the other side of that, a warehouse does not have to look like a warehouse, either! You can jazz up any space if you truly desire to and work at it.

Lastly, he sits down and plans what will go forth from that space. He thinks about what having that space is going to allow his to do. He thinks about the area that he is in and how he can help the community around his by being there. He thinks about whom he will be able to serve to his highest capacity. He contemplates what can and will happen over the course of time.

My challenge for you with this verse is for you to evaluate your current space, if you have one. If you are looking for a space, think about what you need in a space for right now. Use the questions for this verse to help you to get that together! Do not forget to plan what can and will happen!

Questions

1. Is home the best place?
2. Where can I go to work?
3. Do I need and office for what I do?
4. Can I afford office space right now?

7 MAINTAINING THE MAN WITHIN AND WITHOUT

Proverbs 31:17- "She girdeth her loins with strength, and strengtheneth her arms."

A distinguished business man takes care of himself and keeps up his appearance. He exercises regularly and eats well. This is hard to do, yet it is necessary! He has to be ready at a moment's notice, so it is important that he see after his health. Not only are his clients and employees depending on him, his family is also! He has to make sure that what he puts into his body is the best thing for it and does not cause harm!

A distinguished business man gets all necessary health checks and exams. I have known business men who have delayed routine and urgent care health matters because of the down time that may result. My husband is like that. What he had to learn was, at the end of the day, when you are not at your best physically, you are not at your best in any other area! A distinguished business man takes times to himself and recognizes the need to pull back, take a break, and rest. He should have people in place that can take the baton and keep running the race. I know and understand that is not always possible, yet it should be something that he aspires to have.

A distinguished business man's attire is tasteful, professional, and well made. If you are honest, you have seen business men who you have personally wanted to say something to about the way they were dressed. A truly professionally dressed business man can sometimes make those who do not take their attire as seriously feel uncomfortable. It should not be that way – on their end. When it comes to being in the business world, a distinguished business man leads by example!

A distinguished business man maintains the car

he drives. He does not miss oil changes or service checks. He keeps a full gas tank. He does not push his car to its limits and think that he can buy more time. He has full insurance on the car he drives. He keeps his driving record clear. He makes sure the tags are current. He keeps up with car payments. He has roadside assistance, AAA, and a reliable car rental company should anything happen. He keeps the car clean, inside and out. He understands the difference between personal and business mileage while maintaining proper records. He understands that his vehicle is a reflection of him! I do not think I have any more to say about that!

A distinguished business man is in tune with God and has a solid and stable support system. He realizes the importance of having God in his corner and honoring Him! He lets nothing and no one stop him from having his quiet time with God and is known as a man of prayer and fasting if need be! He remembers that the ultimate goal is to please God in all that he does. He realizes that he has to stand before God and give an account of his life, his home, and his business. He makes sure that everything he does is lined up with what God requires. He surrounds himself with like-minded people who will not only help his professionally, but also will point his back to God when it is necessary. He surrounds himself with those who challenge him to do more, go further, and push harder. He surrounds himself with those that will help him to keep his head together, but not make him feel as though he is doing everything wrong.

A distinguished business man spends time strengthening his weak points. He is teachable—this goes back to where we talked about a distinguished man educating himself. He recognizes what he needs help with and asks for it! Whether it is taking care of himself, managing the business, maintaining his vehicle, or even something as simple as creating a social media post—he either researches how to best do it himself or he enlists the help of others. He does not keep up appearances and fakes as if he knows what he is doing, either. He acknowledges what he does not know and sets out to learn so that will never happen again!

For this chapter's questions, I want you to focus on what you are NOT doing and make plans to start going it.

Questions

1. How is my health? How do I dress? What condition is my car in?
2. Is God in His proper place?
3. Am I willing to admit to and strengthen weaknesses?

8 HAVING A GO-GETTER MENTALITY

Proverbs 31:18- "She perceiveth that his merchandise is good: her candle goeth not out by night."

A distinguished business man knows the value of the products and services he offers, but is always looking for ways to improve and serve more people. This means that he stands by the services he provides and can back them up with reputable success stories. He stands by the prices he sets, no matter who may think they are too high or too low. He shows his clients what they will get for the price that they are being asked to pay. This means that the ideas that he presents are original and not the work of someone else – he is not a thief! And, if by chance he IS using someone else's material or ideas, he gives them credit for allowing his to do so. That is where lawsuits and damaged relationships are bred and spiral out of control. It is better to create and have your own! Trust me.

A distinguished business man keeps up with what his competition – if he has any—is doing and adapts without putting himself in the hole. He does not allow the demon of comparison to be fed. He needs to understand that what he has created is good enough to stand toe to toe with what is already out there. He updates his products and services based on market trends that match his core values, the needs of his clients, and newfound knowledge.

A distinguished business man is not afraid to approach his competition and see how they are able to help each other. He believes in networking, even if it is with someone who is in direct competition with him. He understands that sometimes even rivals can help each other. He forms viable and lucrative partnerships after doing his homework on them. He is well informed and well educated about his competition and what they do. He finds those that compliment his services and vice versa.

A distinguished business man works late when it is necessary, especially at the beginning! He sets himself up for success on a daily basis. He makes sure that he has everything he needs to make things happen. That means that those important emails are sent and responses are done. That means that he has made his office supply order. That means that he has planned things out, no matter how loose the plans are. That means that he has confirmed any outside arrangements made with time enough to put plan B into action if necessary.

A distinguished business man sets and maintains high standards and expectations in his business dealings. He comes to the table with his best, not with day old leftover scraps. He puts his best foot forward every day he steps into the workplace. He is ready for whatever comes his way. He expects nothing less than the best out of himself and his employees. He also has a right to have reasonably high expectations of others he has business dealings with, yet understands that those expectations will not always be met. He understands that not everyone he deals with will have the same values and work ethic as he does.

A distinguished business man connects with people who can help him and vice versa. Learning to both give and accept help is important. Whether your business is well establihed or you are just starting out, it is important to network throughout every stage of your business. Go to networking events and present yourself and your business to everyone in there that you know could help propel your business forward. Explain that, although you have just started, you believe in networking while you build. It is important to let the right people know what you are doing because they can help you more than you think they can.

See and understand how important it is to link up with those that you know will help further your goals as a distinguished business man. Understand that you do not have to have it all together in order to do that. Understand that it will eventually help you to get things in order as they needed to be.

A distinguished business man is always looking for opportunities! He pays attention to what he sees and hears around him. He speaks up at the right time and is always ready to do so. He is prepared to start working with someone immediately should that be the case. His preparedness can sometimes be seen as intimidating or even slightly annoying, but his purpose in being that way always becomes clear. He wants whomever he may be speaking with to see that he is the right person to be dealing with in that situation. As I mentioned before, he attends both business and community events where he can get his message out, get his products seen, and potentially get his calendar full. It should get to the point to where he is usually expected to show up at certain events. It should be a shock that he is not there. That comes from people knowing his and what his business is about!

In looking for opportunities, though, a distinguished business man knows that not every opportunity presented to him is one that he should seize. He prays about any opportunity he's considering and does not jump on the first train of the day. He does his homework. He understands that his reputation is on the line and that he cannot be seen working and networking with any and every body out there.

A distinguished business man is a go-getter. He does not wait around for things to come to him. He keeps his ear to the ground and does for himself. He realizes that attitude just might be the driving force behind him getting things done. He knows that things are not going to just fall into his lap. He is going to have to put the work in for what he wants. Yes, he may get a little less sleep. Yes, he may have many headaches. However, he does what is right, pleasing before God, and necessary to get things done.

For this verse's questions, I want you to think about whether or not you have this particular quality. I want you to think about how you exhibit it if you do. If you are not there just yet, make a plan of how you are going to get there and make things happen. A distinguished business man may take his time, but he also knows that time waits for no one!

Questions

1. Am I a go-getter?
2. Do I always present my best?
3. Am I really open to opportunities?
4. Do I take the time to prayerfully consider them?

9 SHINING THE LIGHT

Proverbs 31:19- "She layeth her hands to the spindle, and her hands hold the distaff."

A distinguished business man does things for himself, if he has to, in order to keep his business going! He is very careful with how much he outsources. While outsourcing is necessary, it can be overdone and can become very expensive and more time consuming! He learns how to do what he needs to do when money is an issue. He knows what is out there, but he also knows that he needs to keep his bottom line in tact as well. He will barter should that be feasible, but not every single time he needs something!

A distinguished business man is industrious and hardworking. He is always busy and it may seem to some that he never takes an off day, even when he is taking one! Having a business takes work—work that has to be done by him no matter what. He is not one to take the easy way out and believes in making his work smarter and not harder. He does things in a way that makes his next steps easier to take. He is a man that believes in and understands the importance of preparation. He gives twice as much effort as he expects to receive. He is often criticized for doing too much, yet he knows that it needs to get done. He is intentionally over prepared.

A distinguished business man is both detail and task oriented. He pays attention to the smallest of details and breaks big projects down into manageable tasks with deadlines attached. He makes sure that every T is crossed and every I is dotted. He makes sure that he is prepared for anything that could go wrong. He is thorough, which can be seen as too much for some.

In being detail and task oriented, a distinguished business man makes sure that he does his absolute best. He checks, double checks, and triple checks any written communication that he is sending out to people. He makes sure it is not too wordy, is easy to understand, that it communicates exactly what it needs to, and that it serves the right purpose. He makes sure that it is both eye-catching and appealing, yet still maintains the proper professional tone. He makes sure that he is not being demeaning or condescending in getting his point across. People should be both impressed and informed with anything that they receive from him. What he presents is straightforward and has no gray areas.

A distinguished business man is not afraid to pound the pavement in order to get his name out there. He looks for both traditional and untraditional means of exposure without compromising who he is and what he is trying to get done. I was talking about this in a Facebook group for entrepreneurs. I suggested that we should not rely solely on social media and email to advertise our businesses. Why? There are people that you will not reach that way. A select few in the world still value letters, flyers, and cards. They would much rather get a phone call than a text message.

With that being said, a distinguished business man makes sure that his message gets out across a myriad of avenues. He scouts out the best places to leave information about his business and what he is trying to do. He follows advertising protocols and does not assume that he can put his information out anywhere and everywhere. I have gotten phone calls about leaving information in certain places without asking. Be careful with that!

A distinguished business man makes sure that he stays ahead of the game. He knows what is happening, when, where, how, and who to contact. He makes sure that he is financially ready to get vendor space at events. He makes sure that his marketing materials are noticeable and draw people to him. He is not afraid to offer incentives for working with him, but he does not give too much away. He gives just enough to attract and keep interest.

A distinguished business man knows how to use the tools of his particular trade. He knows his way around a computer. He knows what apps work best for him and he is beyond proficient in using them. He knows how to use any tools and machines that he is around. He always has the best and the latest that is related to his business and understands the value of upgrading when it is time to do so. He does his research throughout the process of using anything. He looks for tools that will lead to his being more productive. As previously stated, he makes sure that he has all necessary supplies. If he finds himself in a time crunch, he knows where to go to get things done in the time needed.

A distinguished business man's sleeves are always rolled up and he is ready to work at any given time.

When there is a crisis, a big deadline, or a big event coming, the distinguished business man prays to God for help and strength and then he puts his hands on something. He is known as someone who is willing to work hard, is willing to step in and help, is both dependable and reliable, and sets the bar high when it comes to working and helping others.

For this chapter and verse's questions, I want you to think about where you are right now. Would these things be said of you? What is stopping that from happening? What can you do to rectify that? Take this time to really think about that.

Questions

1. Would these things be said of me?
2. What is stopping these things from being said about me?
3. What can I do to rectify this and to have these things to be said of me?

10 BEING OTHERS MINDED

Proverbs 31:20—"She stretcheth her hand to the poor; yea, she reacheth forth her hand to the needy."

A distinguished business man looks for ways to help the community through his business without giving too much away. Did we not talk about this already? Yes, but this time we are going to look at it from a different angle.

A distinguished business man prayerfully participates in events hosted by organizations that he supports. His affiliations are clear, as are his reasons for having those affiliations. This is a two-edged sword at times because there will be someone somewhere who will take issue with who and what he chooses to support; however, he cannot allow that to influence him. As we said before, it is not meant for us to work and link up with everyone we encounter. Not every cause is one that we should support. He is criticized for supporting organizations that may be seen as old-fashioned, outdated, and antiquated. He may be accused of being close-minded and told that he needs to broaden his spectrum of thinking.

On the other hand, there will be those who are glad to have him supporting and endorsing them. These organizations are looking for people who are not scared to go against the grain and stick with those causes and organizations that are time tested and approved. He is not quick to support something new, either. He has to see results before putting his name behind it. He realizes that whom he allows himself to affiliate with can make his or break him in some instances. He is also not afraid to lose clientele that take issue with who he supports. He supports those that line up with his business convictions and values. More importantly, he supports those that line up with God!

A distinguished business man is visible, involved, and vocal in the communities surrounding both his home and his business. People know and are comfortable with him and know that he will stand for what is right, even when that position is unpopular. He is known as someone who speaks up for those who cannot speak up for themselves and holds those in power around him accountable. He does his part in making the community safe. His neighbors and colleagues are happy to know him. He is approachable and takes time to listen to the concerns of those that come to him for help. He is able to recognize something out of the ordinary and take action without endangering himself.

A distinguished business man volunteers his time when things happen. Not every problem can be solved while sitting behind a desk! He puts on that company t-shirt (or not) and goes to where he is needed. He does not show up emptyhanded, either.

He may not know exactly what is needed, but he walks into the situation with something in hand. He is ready to help, even if the work is going to be hard.

The smallest gestures can lead to better and greater later. Think about that as you answer the questions for this chapter and verse. How are you seen in your community?

Questions

1. How can my business help the community?
2. What organizations should I support (or not)?
3. Is my business known for helping out?

11 MAKE WAY FOR THE BEST

Proverbs 31:21—"She is not afraid of the snow for her household: for all her household are clothed with scarlet."

Now, we are going to approach this one two ways: family and business, with family being first. A distinguished business man makes sure that when the seasons change, his family is prepared for it. His children have good, sturdy cold weather clothing that fits. They have hats, gloves, and whatever else is needed to help them during the winter months. He makes sure that what they are eating gives them energy and is filling. He scouts out alternative routes to get them to school and stays on top of school closings. If he homeschools his children, he makes sure that they have everything they need at home to continue their learning. He keeps an eye on sensitive areas at home and sees that they are protected.

Now for the business part. A distinguished business man has his employees in a safe and comfortable working environment with thought for the weather. He has a fair inclement weather policy and does not expect his employees to brave hazardous conditions to get to work. He makes a way for them to work from home if possible. He checks in on them and their families to make sure that they are okay and have what they need. When the summer months come, he makes sure to limit the time they are outside and is aware of heat advisories. If they have to be outside, he makes sure that they stay fed, stay hydrated, and take needed breaks.

The building that the distinguished business man's employees work in is well maintained and prepared for the weather. When his employees come to work, it is not the same temperature in the building as it is outside. They are able to work at their highest productivity levels because they are comfortable. When there is a severe weather threat, his employees are able to find a place of safety and are allowed to check on their loved ones. He provides for them if they end up being shut in or locked down for any reason.

A distinguished business man provides weather appropriate uniforms for those that need it and a flexible, yet professional, dress code for others. The uniforms that he provides are well made and hold up to the weather. They are not too thick nor too thin. He has his employees' best interest at heart. He makes sure that what he provides will help them to do their job to the best of their ability.

A distinguished business man makes sure that the vehicles and tools that his employees use are ready for the weather as well! He makes sure that nothing is going to break down because it was not properly maintained. Anyone who drives a company vehicle will have air and heat in the vehicle. They will not have to worry about breaking down somewhere because vehicle maintenance was not done.

A distinguished business man has happy employees. They enjoy working for him because they know that they matter to him. They are willing to give extra effort because he shows them that they are valuable to him. They feel as though he is in tune with what they need and does not expect them to do anything that he would not do. He takes care of those who are injured or have weather related incidents to occur. They know he will not expect them to keep working through a weather related health issue. He will get them the medical attention that is necessary!

There is not too much more I can say here, so I will leave you to the questions for this chapter. Think about the policies that you have in place in your business. If they are not in place, it is time to make a plan. If you have a plan that is not working, it is time to revamp that plan. Do not be afraid to ask your employees what they need to get their jobs done during those weather changes.

Questions

1. Is my business ready for the weather?
2. Have I done a family purge and purchase?
3. Do my employees have what they need for those rough weather days?

12 YOU ARE WHAT YOU WEAR

Proverbs 31:22- "She maketh herself coverings of tapestry; her clothing is silk and purple."

A distinguished business man has a flexible wardrobe and dresses for the occasion at hand. He does not show up to a community clean up event in a business suit and dress shoes! His clothing is well made and not too flamboyant. He knows when to dress up, dress down, or dress to the nines!

A distinguished business man is conscious of what he wears at all times. He does not wear certain things to work simply because he can. He realizes that he has set expectations and abides by them himself. He does not come to work in something that violates policy. Again, he leads by example. He also watches how he wears his hair. The whole point of this is to say that he does not draw unnecessary attention to himself. The way that he looks should not be the sole focus of the day.

A distinguished business man dresses with a sense of dignity and professionalism. We can all come up with an example of someone coming to work in something they should not have worn in a work environment. He should not change because people around him are uncomfortable, either. He should serve as an example to those around him.

One thing that I was told in a workshop once was that, if you doubted how you were supposed to dress for a job, watch your boss. A distinguished business man should be someone who those under his can pattern themselves after in this area. You can go overboard with it, so be careful. How can you go overboard? I will tell you.

A distinguished business man would not expect his employees to dress in the same way he does. Let me explain. While he might make recommendations or give advice, he has to understand that they may not be possible for all of his employees. They may not make enough to shop where he shops. The material he wears may not look the same way on them. The color he wears may not be right for them. This is what happens when you have unrealistic expectations.

A distinguished business man does not have a double standard in his dress. We have talked about that some already, but let us go a little further. He does not have the "'Do as I say and not as I do" mentality with his employees. Again, he does not wear something that violates the policy that he put in case nor does he reprimand someone that does the same on the same day. In other words, he cannot come to work in a muscle shirt and jeans and then tell another employee that he has to go home and change. Nine times out of ten that employee is going to call his out as well. His response should not be that he is the boss and he can do what he wants. That causes confusion and then people start to think that way every time they see him.

Double standards are dangerous in business and in other areas as well! A distinguished business man cannot come in looking as though he stepped off a magazine cover while his employees barely have what they need, when the uniforms are company issued, in order to be in accordance with the dress code. That tells his employees that he is more important than they are and that they will just have to deal with that they are given. Having that kind of mentality breeds contempt and leads to low productivity among employees. It also causes a breakdown in the employer-employee relationship.

I know some have tried to account for this by having a separate dress code policy for management level and entry-level employees. Even with that in mind, a distinguished business man still watches what he wears and should not have a bad attitude about someone telling him he could be take more care in what he chose to wear on a particular day.

I have seen it too many times! Differences were made when they should not have been made. A distinguished business man does not use his position to excuse his actions, his dress, his work ethic, or his demeanor. I am going to leave you with that.

My challenge to you in this chapter is to take a good long look at yourself and what you have in your closet. Ask yourself what you would do if an employee came to work dressed as you were. Be objective in that, too, and be honest. Although you are in a higher position, you are being watched just as you are watching others.

Questions

1. Do I need to purge?
2. Do I have a double standard?
3. Is my dress code realistic?

13 HIS EMPIRE—HIS EMPIRE

Proverbs 31:23- "Her husband is known in the gates, when he sitteth among the elders of the land."

A distinguished business man uses his business to help exalt his wife. Huh? He does WHAT? Let me explain. He creates opportunities for his wife to use her skills in his business and gives her credit for her contributions. Even though the business is "yours," there should be allowances for her to contribute. You know what she can do. You know what she is good at. Give her the chance to flex her muscles and show her skills. When people you interact with meet her, they should already know about her and that can lead to side opportunities for her. Think about that for a second.

When someone asks you what your wife does, what do you say? Let me just warn you now and tell you to watch what you say! Whether she has a job, is a stay at home mom, or is an entrepreneur herself, watch how you speak of her! It will get back to her, no matter how harmless the comment was.

One thing I love about my husband is that he tells anyone who asks everything that I do. He has the books that I've written in his office library and encourages his colleagues to read them!

A distinguished business man may have his wife as his first client, depending on the scope of his business. He is doing more than bouncing ideas off of her – he is helping her to start something of his own or helping her in the job that she currently has. He uses what he has learned to help her to get ahead in what she is doing.

Again, a distinguished business man uses his skills to help his wife build her entrepreneurial dreams. He is not stingy with what he learns nor does he treat her differently from any other client. Yes, he is dealing with his wife, but she should receive the same level of effort that he would give another client. The only difference that should exist is whether he charges her or not, which is between the two of them. He realizes that in helping her, he is also helping himself. His wife can help his to fine tune his pitches, revise his approach, and come up with new ideas. This should be the safest client relationship of all! This should be the most fulfilling. This one should get the most effort.

My husband is an event planner at heart. Since I am always going to some kind of event, he helps me by creating my table set up. He helps with color schemes, product placement, and even proofreads fliers! He even decorated my office! That is just an example.

A distinguished business man is supportive of his wife's career and entrepreneurial pursuits, which can sometimes cause a conflict. However, he and his wife should find common ground so that neither one of them is forced to give up what they are doing for the sake of the other. This is not an easy thing to do! Schedules get crossed, emergencies come up, and things happen. That is why it is important that the distinguished business man makes sure that he and his wife stay on the same page at all times.

A distinguished business man has his wife's best business interests at heart. He does not do anything to undermine her business nor intentionally bring it down. He does not allow her business successes to make him jealous and cloud his judgment. He does not refuse to help her if things are moving faster and doing better in her business than in his at the time. He does not refer her to subpar people to get business needs met. He does not withhold information that will keep her from making a bad business decision. He does not leave her on her own. He does small things behind the scenes to help her, even when she does not want him to and says she has it together. He pays attention to the things she looks over and makes sure that it is not needed. He does not say that he does not have time to help her because he is too busy.

As hard as it may be, a distinguished business man realizes that her career or entrepreneurship is just as important as his is and that she deserves the same – if not more—support than she gives him. He understands that it is not all about him and is willing to share the stage with his wife without feeling as if he is being slighted. He makes it his business to professionally coexist with his wife. He prays for her and her business. He recommends her to those who may need her. He lets her know about events that are going on that are relevant to her. He helps her to keep her calendar straight, among other things. He makes sure that whatever he does for his business, he does for hers! When she has a special event, he is there and gives his undivided attention and effort. At that moment, he is all about her and what she has going on. He is the epitome of a strong united front for her.

Your questions for this challenge are simple—think about how you can help your wife!

Questions

1. How can I help my wife through my business?
2. How can I professionally coexist with her?
3. Who am I linked up with that can help her?
4. How can I best support her?
5. How do I treat her as a client?

14 ESTABLISHING YOUR REPUTATION

Proverbs 31:24- "She maketh fine linen, and selleth it; and delivereth girdles unto the merchant."

A distinguished business man always has quality products, inventory on hand, and is ready to sell at a moment's notice. He is prepared to both talk about and demonstrate his product or service, is knowledgeable about what he offers, and speaks about it in a way that earns his a client contract or sale. He is not pushy, obnoxious, or forceful, nor does he appear to be a know-it-all. He knows how to present his business and skill set with confidence and professional decorum. He watches his body language when communicating with a potential client. He mentally checks his attitude and his demeanor as well. He is conscious of how he is coming across in the conversation and is willing to quickly correct himself when needed. His goal is to make sure that the person talking to his leaves the conversation with a good vibe about him.

A distinguished business man delivers his products quickly and promptly. That means that his clients get what they were promised, when they were promised, how they were promised, and at the price they were promised. He is not one to risk his professional reputation over being tired, overconfident, nor complacent. He takes every order and appointment seriously. His clients know him as someone who does what he says he is going to do. He stays in constant communication with everyone involved to insure that things are handled properly and takes care of it when it is not.

A distinguished business man makes he that he has enough supplies for whatever he is endeavoring to do. He knows who, what, when, where, why, how, and how much. He has a backup plan when he does not have access to his go-to people. He has done his homework and develops tunnel vision when it is necessary. He focuses on the task that hand and is not easily distracted. He sometimes over prepares on purpose!

Getting back to the matter at hand, a distinguished business man orders necessary items in a timely manner. He doesn't look at his planner, see an event coming up, and say that he doesn't have to do it today because he has time. A statement like that will be his undoing. Why? It is because things happen! The item he needs may be backordered. A storm system could come in that would delay his order. Worst of all, what he orders could not arrive until after the event for which it was needed! This is not a chance that a distinguished business man takes. If he has any doubt at all, he does something about that. He calls the merchant to make sure that it is in stock and does not rely on what he sees on their website. He checks with shipping companies to see if there is anything going on that could delay his order. He, again, has a plan B should he not be able to do things the exact way that he planned! Think about that for a minute.

A distinguished business man has people in place to help ensure that things are done properly. He knows that sometimes being a one-man show is just not possible, feasible, or healthy! He knows whom he can count on and he compensates them fairly. He does not undervalue them. He refuses to allow them to work for free. He takes care of them. He listens to them and realizes that they are there to help and not to change everything about his business. He understands that they are there so that all he has to do is serve his clients and not worry about all the behind the scenes stuff.

My brother and I have this very arrangement. Anytime he has a speaking engagement that involves book sales, I am there. He hates it when I do that, but I do not care! He knows that all I want him to do is walk in the door, speak, and sign the books that have been purchased. What do I do? I make sure that there are no blank spots on the table. I make sure that I stay logged in to his payment software and that the connection is strong where I am. I have my laptop and iPad out and on his author's page on Amazon for those who want to order their books online. Does he take care of me? Yes, he does! How? He speaks up for me while I'm busy working, meaning that he lets people know who I am, what I do, and that I'm an author as well. He lets me know about upcoming events that are relevant to me. If someone comes to him that he cannot help, he will send them my way. Not to mention he pays for gas, parking, food, and my time! Would your team say this about you?

A distinguished business man trains his employees well enough to be able to speak in his stead! I cannot stress enough how important this is! "I don't know" should never be a part of any of your team members' or employees' vocabulary. He makes sure that they can answer questions about his products and services. They should not have to run to him for help with answering simple questions. They should only have to come to him when it is a matter that everyone knows that he needs to handle.

A distinguished business man follows up with clients and takes care of issues promptly. This is major when it comes to client relationships. His clients want to know that they will not be abandoned once the money is paid and the service is done. They want to know that he is going to check on them and offer additional assistance in the future or just to find out how things are going. For example, I check on my clients every two weeks!

Think about this as you work on the questions for this chapter and verse. Think about what you need to revamp, revise, or improve!

Questions

1. How prepared am I to sell? Do I have inventory on hand?
2. Am I using the best means to deliver my products?
3. Can my team work without me?
4. How is my customer service?

15 BE YOUR OWN REWARD

Proverbs 31:25-"Strength and honour are her clothing; and she will rejoice in time to come."

A distinguished business man does not need constant recognition in order to feel successful. He focuses on both the work and the reward. He realizes that sometimes the work itself is the reward! He understands and sees the value in a smiling customer's face. The feeling that comes from knowing that he has given them what they need can be just as fulfilling.

A distinguished business man understands that results are not always immediate! Although it can be frustrating, he knows that things can take more time and more effort. He understands that he may have a client that he never hears from again, but he will see something about them later on that will make him smile. He understands that he may have only been a seed planter to that client. They got what they needed from him for the moment and went on to work with someone else. However, he can still rejoice because it all started with him. This principle was very evident in the life of the Apostle Paul! I Corinthians 3:6,7 says-" I have planted, Apollos watered, but God gave the increase. So then neither is he that planted any thing, neither he that watereth; but God that giveth the increase." The distinguished business man understands that and is able to move forward without any resentment.

A distinguished business man knows that not every encounter will turn into a business deal or sale. We just talked about that! He is not meant to work with everyone and not everyone is meant to work with him. He understands that he offers something of value, yet not to everyone. I hear people say all the time that they were not a good fit for someone. The same is true for the distinguished business man. Although this may be the case, he goes a step further and refers them to someone who may be a better fit for them. He does not just leave them to their own devices. He still helps.

A distinguished business man does not work in order to be considered for awards or memberships in professional organizations. He does not dismiss these things, yet he realizes there is much more at stake. He works in spite of and seeks to please the Lord before anyone else! Although he may be judged unfairly by not being affiliated with certain organizations, he does not jump up and apply just to gain clientele. Remember how we talked about the distinguished business man prayerfully considering whom he links up with? This is what I mean. And, it is important to note that some of these so-called "professional organizations" are not worth their name. Some of them are simply looking to recruit and have nothing real to offer. Some even go so far as to ask that you pay for the award that they say you "won." The distinguished business man does not fall for that.

A distinguished business man knows that his day is coming and looks to God to open doors for him! He knows how important it is to do things in God's timing, that promotion comes from Him, and that it will come so long as he is doing what is right and pleasing before Him. He also knows the difference between what comes from God and what does not. He does not fall for every good thing that comes towards him. He recognizes when things come with strings attached. He knows when things are too good to be true. He pays attention to what has happened to others who have gone down that road. He is not easily attracted by notoriety.

A distinguished business man knows how to be his own reward! Think about it. Think about the day that you met all of the goals and deadlines that you had and how good you felt about it. You wanted to do a little something for yourself and there is nothing wrong with that. You maybe left early that day or took a much needed and deserved vacation. You may go to eat at a restaurant that you have wanted to try out. You bought yourself something you had your eye on. Or, you did something for the business that you had been putting off because you were so busy. You maybe even did something for someone else! The possibilities are fun to consider and endless. He is his own motivation. He is his own cheering squad. And, he is okay with that!

As you work through the questions for this chapter and verse, think about what rewards drive you. Think about what you would want. Think about what you would do for yourself when given the chance. Think about the doors that God has opened you!

Questions

1. What rewards motivate me?
2. What type of rewards do I want?
3. What would I do for myself if and when I'm

given the chance?

4. What doors has God already opened? What doors am I looking for God to open?

16 KEEP YOURSELF IN CHECK

Proverbs 31:26- "She openeth her mouth with wisdom; and in her tongue is the law of kindness."

A distinguished business man not only knows what he's talking about, but also knows how to talk to people! We can all remember a time when we have not liked the way in which someone spoke to us. It was not what they said – it was how they said it.

A distinguished business man watches how he speaks to people. He does not talk down to people as if they are beneath him. I have had this happen to me and had to watch how I responded. He does not speak to people as if they know nothing of what he's talking about. He will be surprised the moment that he does because he just may find out something about the subject that he did not know.

A distinguished business man knows how to

agree to disagree without taking it personally. This is something that many business man struggle with—disagreement. We are prone to see it as something that we did or said wrong that caused the situation to end as it did. He understands that not everyone will see things his way, no matter how right he may be. He may know that he is right. Those to whom he is speaking may know he is right, yet that does not mean that they are going to admit it, either. He knows how to gracefully and tactfully end any disagreement and is mindful of his emotions and tone as well.

A distinguished business man can keep his composure under pressure. He is not hot headed nor quick tempered. He can sometimes be seen as nonchalant and uncaring, which is not the case at all. He knows how to handle himself and deals with his personal feelings in private. No one in the room will know that he is shaken unless it is something dire. Even then, he is able to remain poised and level headed, which is not an easy thing to do at all, but he learns how to do it.

A distinguished business man is an active listener. He listens to understand and not to rebut or respond. We have all had times where we have started responding to what someone said only to have them to tell us that we were not listening to what they said. A distinguished business man listens and considers everything that is said to him before he answers. People will think that he is not listening; that is, until he responds! He allows the speaker to finish their complete thought and then asks them if they are done speaking. It is then that he communicates his side of the issue with tact, respect, and clarity. He makes sure that he is not misunderstood.

A distinguished business man speaks to build up and not to tear down. This is very important for any business man that has employees. He knows how to get his point across and it not be mistaken as harsh.

That comes from having a good rapport with those he employs, yet it is not an easy thing to establish. He can deliver bad news in a good way and still maintain the integrity of the relationship. He may even over explain why it is being said and what needs to be done after it has been said. He does that because he wants the person to still feel as though they are a vital part of the organization. Does this apply to terminating someone also? Yes, it does. He knows how to point out the reason for the termination without making it personal and without attacking the person. When he is asked about this person, he does not automatically begin to speak negatively of them. He highlights what they did that worked well while he employed them and discusses the issues that they had in a professional tone.

A distinguished business man maintains a professional demeanor in his speech and communication. He knows when to be serious and when to be laid back. He respects the position of the person to whom he is speaking. For example, he does not speak to an elected official as if he or he was someone he met on the street, even if he knows them personally. He does not use a lot of slang when speaking to people. The fact that he endeavors to speak properly at all times can annoy people who are not used to that. He would much rather be known as someone who is articulate.

A distinguished business man is clear in what he says and makes sure it is understood. If he is a father, he already knows how this goes. He knows that there will be people who are not really listening while he is talking. He will then say something that he knows will bring them back into the conversation. He will purposely ask the same question ten different ways to make sure that he is being understood. He will send an email reminding the listeners of what was talked about previously. He will repeat himself when necessary and will not care that people are annoyed by it. He may even go so far as to record himself in case of a chronic misunderstanding.

A distinguished business man is not easily drawn into drama and frivolous arguments. He understands that he does not have to get involved in every conversation that comes his way. He can sense when to back away from a conversation. He stays out of conversations he should not be involved in. He recognizes when he needs to intervene. He is capable of keeping business and personal matters separate and addresses them at the appropriate times.

A distinguished business man thinks before he speaks. He questions what he is about to say. He makes sure that he is going to say it in the best possible way. He thinks about whether or not it should even be said. He plans how he is going to say it, especially if he is upset. He is laughed at because he has often seen talking to himself. He knows that he needs to do that in order to keep his head straight. He prays and asks God for wisdom and guidance in what to say and how to say it, which takes us into the questions for this verse.

Think about ways you can communicate better. Do those to whom you speak see you as a voice of reason and wisdom or do they hate to see you coming? Work on that.

Questions

1. How do I handle conflict?
2. How do I come off in professional and private conversations?
3. What are people saying about the way I talk to them?

17 PRODUCTIVELY BUSY

Proverbs 31:27- "She looketh well to the ways of her household, and eateth not the bread of idleness."

A distinguished business man does not sit back and watch everyone else do what needs to be done! He is not annoyed when he is asked to help get something done. He understands that his reputation is at stake and that people talk. He knows how important it is for people to be able to put a face to the name.

When it comes to his home life, he is busy when he is at home. He is checking to make sure that his wife and children have everything that they need. He is doing whatever needs to be done in order for his home to run smoothly. He sits down and talks to his family. He prays with and for them. He makes sure that his relationships are solid!

A distinguished business man checks to make sure that he and everyone else around him has what they need to get the job done. He accepts the blame when this does not happen. He does not try to put it on anyone else, even if he gave someone else the responsibility. He knows that anything that happens in his business is a direct reflection of his. He makes sure that, once his team comes in, they can get right to work and the project can be finished on time. He makes sure that no one is scrambling around trying to find supplies or figure out what to do.

A distinguished business man steps in to help when and where he is needed. He does not carry himself as though he is too good to work. He does not tell people that he pays them to do those things. He may be busy at the time, but he finds a way to be involved in both situations. He may wear himself thin, but he rests in the fact that his team knows that they can count on him to not just be another pretty face. He wants to be known as someone who is willing to work!

A distinguished business man is always busy doing something pertaining to the business. Some may say that he is not doing anything, but others trust that he is much busier than what he appears to be. He might be in front of three computer screens and on the phone at the same time, but the results are soon clear. He may not be in the office all day every day, but the reason is soon revealed. He may always been seen on TV or heard on the radio, but it is all about the business and how he can help it to grow. He may be in meetings from sunup to sundown, but that means that important business decisions are being made and vital partnerships are being formed. He may be sending a million emails, but it could result in everyone being helped and/or in the business making more money! He may never sit down and it may be because, if he does, something will not get done.

A distinguished business man checks on his

employees' personal and professional well-being. He takes time out of his day to sit and talk to each person that works for him.

A distinguished business man pays attention to everything and responds promptly. He does not sit back and wait to see if things are going to blow up before he says or does anything. He gets up and keeps that from happening. If he sees trouble coming, he is there standing in front of it. He solves what appears to be a problem before it becomes one. He does not wait for things to go wrong. He is so vigilant that sometimes he scares people, which is not a bad thing because that means they know that they need to be about business at all times. His employees know that he is watching and knows everything that goes on. Think about a time when you have done something that you thought your boss did not see—only to end up in their office talking about that very issue!

Lastly, a distinguished business man does not

delegate for the purpose of sitting back with his feet up. He delegates because he needs help, to give others an opportunity to shine and show what they can do, to keep from snapping or breaking down, and to keep from quitting.

How are you using this verse? Are you using this verse? It is time to reflect on that now.

Questions

1. Do I micromanage?
2. Do I delegate? If so, why and how do I do it?

18 CROWN OF HIS FAMILY

Proverbs 31:28- "Her children arise up, and call her blessed; her husband also, and he praiseth her."

A distinguished business man has the love and support of his family! They are his first line of defense and the foundation of his support system. He works with them in mind and understands that everything that he says, does, and thinks affects them. He is careful not to get so bogged down with business that they are left stranded. They are his biggest cheerleaders!

A distinguished business man is an example to his children. He behaves and carries himself in the way that he expects his children to. He does not do things in front of them for show—they can see through that! He shows them the value in hard work, how to properly spend money, and the importance of balance. Most importantly, he shows them a genuine walk and relationship with the Lord—they see Him working in their home and in his business. He leads by example.

A distinguished business man instills a sense of entrepreneurship in his children. He recognizes their gifts and talents early and cultivates them. He teaches them business principles on their level. He involves them in what he is doing. He finds ways for them to use their gifts and talents. He helps them to start their own businesses, even at a young age. He uses what he has learned to help them to grow and expand their thinking. He looks for a place in his business for what they have created. He channels their educational path based on their goals, which is not always easy to do. He helps them to read and research what it takes for them to do what they want to do. More importantly, he helps them to seek God's will for their lives in using those gifts and talents.

A distinguished business man, again, has a

business that utilizes the gifts and talents that his family possesses. Why do I keep talking about this? It is because this is something that I really want you to take the time to consider. You could be missing the person that could do better work than who you are about to pay. You may be about to endure a lot of frustration that could be avoided simply by letting your family help you. Do not sleep on the gifts and talents that are present in your family. Unearth them and put them to use!

A distinguished man conducts himself in a manner that makes his family look good. In other words, no one is going to come back to his wife talking about what they saw him doing. He operates with thoughts of how his family would feel if they found out he didn't do things in the best way. He never does anything that would embarrass his wife. His wife is able to defend his personal and professional actions without being laughed at because of something that everyone knows except her. This goes back to when we talked about his wife being able to trust him. He has to be careful of what he does both in public and in private.

Lastly, and again, a distinguished business man's family knows that they come first. They know that they are important to him. He includes them. He cares for them. He shows that they matter. He is not working during family time. He calls home frequently when he is away. He is present in his child's school and at school events. It has to be a matter of national security for his to miss anything going on in his family life. He has balance.

For this chapter's questions, I want you to evaluate yourself.

Questions

1. What can you do to make sure that your family is taken care of and is not missing me?
2. Do I encourage my family to use their gifts and talents?

19 NO LESS THAN EXCELLENCE

Proverbs 31:29-"Many daughters have done virtuously, but thou excellest them all."

A distinguished business man strives for excellence! He does not take his position in his home nor in the world lightly. He understands how important it is do things in the best way. He understands that he has to give everything his best effort. He does not cut corners. He is not extremely cheap, yet he does not overspend. He understands the power of customer reviews. He strives to make sure that he gives the services and provides the products that he would want to receive. He wants people to recommend him!

A distinguished business man is cognizant of others who have paved the way for him and builds on the legacies they set. He understands that he is where he is because of the efforts of other people.

Although he has broken through some barriers in his entrepreneurial journey, he knows that there are other men who fought and clawed for that to happen. He knows the history of the industrious men of the Bible and of those in world history. He sets out to leave a legacy that others behind him will want to follow themselves. He realizes that people are looking to him to set the standard and he sets it high, yet not so high that it can never be met.

A distinguished business man, as we just said, realizes how important it is to be an example and to inspire others! He builds a business that is unique, yet somewhat easy to replicate. He uses what he learns to help others. He does not see those who want to learn as competition. He realizes that this person may be able to help someone that he may not be able to reach in his business. He establishes a support network and seeks to help other men who want to take that first crucial entrepreneurial step. He is raw, honest, and real in his counsel. He helps them to understand their value in the sight of God and others. He helps them to establish businesses that generate revenue and lead to goals being met. He reproduces himself as many times as he can before his time is done!

A distinguished business man gives his best, does his best, works with the best, and produces the best. Let us talk about each one of those in detail. First, he gives his best—he is not haphazard or lazy in his dealings. He doesn't simply do what it takes to get by. He is not one that pacifies his clients; he genuinely serves them. He does not throw something together and expect for them to be okay with it simply because of who he is.

Next, he does his best—not the same as giving his best. When he does his best, he does not find himself wishing that he had done more or done better. He is not sitting back and hoping that they are not negatively impacted by his lack of effort. He uses the best of materials in putting things together because he would want things to be done that way for him. He uses his ace materials and resources when called upon to help.

Then, he works with the best. While he tries to help those who are getting their businesses off the ground, he knows that quality comes with having a good track record. He is willing to invest a little more in working with someone who produces the results that he is looking for. He does his research on people and makes sure that they are a good fit for his business and the project at hand.

Last, he produces the best! He, again, creates what he would want to receive. He charges a price that he would be willing to pay if the situation were reversed, yet he does not just give his products away. He creates something of value that has a high demand. He revamps and refines what he already has out there when needed. He is always learning and looking for better ways to produce things. He is always in somebody's workshop or webinar learning a new skill that will help push his business to greater heights. Remember what we said about striving for excellence? That is a big part of it.

For this chapter, I want you to think about excellence. I want you to look at what you have created and ask yourself if you did that with a sense of urgency and feeling of excellence. If not, think about what you need to revamp and tweak, even if it is already out there. People revise and revamp things all the time. There is nothing wrong with doing better once you learn better, so get after it!

Questions

1. Am I actively striving for excellence?
2. Do I appreciate what others went through for me to be where I am now?
3. Am I being inspiring and being a light to others?
4. Am I putting out my best work?

20 GOD-FEARING BUSINESS MAN

Proverbs 31:30- "Favour is deceitful, and beauty is vain: but a woman that feareth the Lord, she shall be praised."

We are coming to the end of our time together. If I had to pick one thought that was the most important, it would be this one.

A distinguished business man is known as a man of faith! He shares his faith with all that he comes into contact with—he lets them know that his business is built on his faith. When he is asked why he does things a certain way, he responds with what God's word says about the matter. He is not afraid to start a meeting with prayer. He communicates the value of having God in his life and his business. He will be shunned and ridiculed. He may lose clients and money. However, he knows that God will provide because he stood firm in his faith and trust in Him!

A distinguished business man keeps God at the forefront of his business. He does nothing without prayer. He looks for answers in God's word. Before he does anything, he thinks about whether or not God would be pleased with that he is about to do. He has reminders around him that help to keep his on God's track for his life and business. He is always before God for his family, business, employees, and clients.

A distinguished business man seeks to honor the Lord in all that he does in his business. He does not do business with any and every one. He operates by his core convictions, even when it costs him. His business is built and run on Biblical principles. He is not going to do anything in his business that is contrary to God's will or God's way. What God thinks of his business is important to him!

A distinguished business man does not allow business to get in the way of his relationship with the Lord. He is not going to schedule a meeting or business matter of any kind at a time when he would be in church, if he can avoid it. He is in church if he is traveling. He gets his quiet time in with God before he starts his day. God is his first choice and not his last resort. He does not enter into a business partnership that is scripturally wrong, no matter how much money he stands to make from it!

A distinguished business man PRAYS! He begins and ends his day with prayer. He is annoying to people at times because he tells them that he has to pray before he can give them an answer. His business and family are immersed in prayer daily. There is never a time when he will not pray about a matter. He does not assume that anything is okay to do without praying first.

A distinguished business man cares about how God feels and what His word says about a given issue. He may read everything he gets his hands on in order to find a solution to his problem—and he may find one—yet, he will still pick up his Bible and ask God to show his how to deal with the situation in light of scripture. He understands the importance of consulting God and His word in both major and minor decisions. He, again, wants to do things in a way that is right and pleasing to God. He wants Him to be pleased in all that he endeavors and desires to do. He does not take Him, His word, nor His wisdom for granted.

Lastly, a distinguished business man understands that good stewardship is a part of business and that God will hold his accountable for it. He realizes that he will have to answer both on earth and in Heaven for every decision he has made in his business. This drives him to make sure that he does both what is right and what is best in the eyes of God. He is not wasteful, slothful, or lazy; nor is he sneaky, conniving, or underhanded. He is not disrespectful nor rude and does things legally. He is a person of personal and professional integrity. He understands that the vision for his business came from God and He is entrusting him with it. He understands that he is His manager of what He has allowed his to build.

In the questions for this chapter, I want you to think about God's place in your business.

Questions

1. Does God have a place in my business? Where?
2. Am I known known as a man of faith? If not, how can I make that happen?
3. If I am known as a man of faith, am I using and showing that every day?
4. Am I operating in light of the vision that God has for me or am I looking at it and doing things the way I want to do them?

21 JUST SMILE AND WAVE

Proverbs 31:31-"Give her of the fruit of his hands; and let her own works praise his in the gates."

A distinguished business man lets his work speak for him. He also speaks highly of what he does, yet without bragging or boasting. Huh? You can speak well of yourself without coming across as arrogant or cocky. There is a difference between that and confidence. Think about it!

A distinguished business man has testimonials from those who have received his services. He can think that he is the best, yet his words are empty if he does not have any proof behind them. His testimonials are not fabricated, either. He knows that what he is doing may be new. Even if he is his own first client, he has something to show for the work that he does.

A distinguished business man produces goods and services that speak for themselves. Sometimes, he will not have to do any talking at all. When people look at his offerings, they know exactly what they are getting and he will be standing there smiling. They ask and answer their own questions, simply by looking at what he has put together for them.

A distinguished business man has a benefit statement that entails what you can expect to receive from his company. You will know why he is the right person for the job. People will understand exactly what he is trying to do for them. They see the benefit in working with him. When they are cycling through comparisons in their minds, his company will still come to the forefront of their thoughts! He draws them in without saying a word!

Lastly, a distinguished business man pays himself well without putting his business in jeopardy! How many times have you heard about companies going bankrupt because the owner could not get a handle on their personal spending with business funds? Exactly! A distinguished business man would rather not take a salary from his business rather than destroy it. He creates multiple income streams and protects his business income in case of emergencies. He has a contingency plan for himself if he cannot take a salary from the business.

This last chapter is short because, as fun as this has been, it is the end of our journey through Proverbs 31. For this chapter's questions, I really want you to think about whether or not you are doing this and what you need to do for this to happen. It is time to pray, ponder, and plan!

It is my hope and prayer that this journey has been beneficial for you. We have talked about many things that many men do not think about and are not willing to do. I wish you God's best in all that you do and create!

Questions

1. What does my work say to others? Do I like what it's saying?
2. Is my benefit statement true, visible, straight forward, and easy to understand?
3. How do I pay myself?
4. Am I taking steps to become a Distinguished Business Man?

www.ingramcontent.com/pod-product-compliance
Lightning Source LLC
Chambersburg PA
CBHW071445180526
45170CB00001B/473